LONDON

SHOPS & MORE

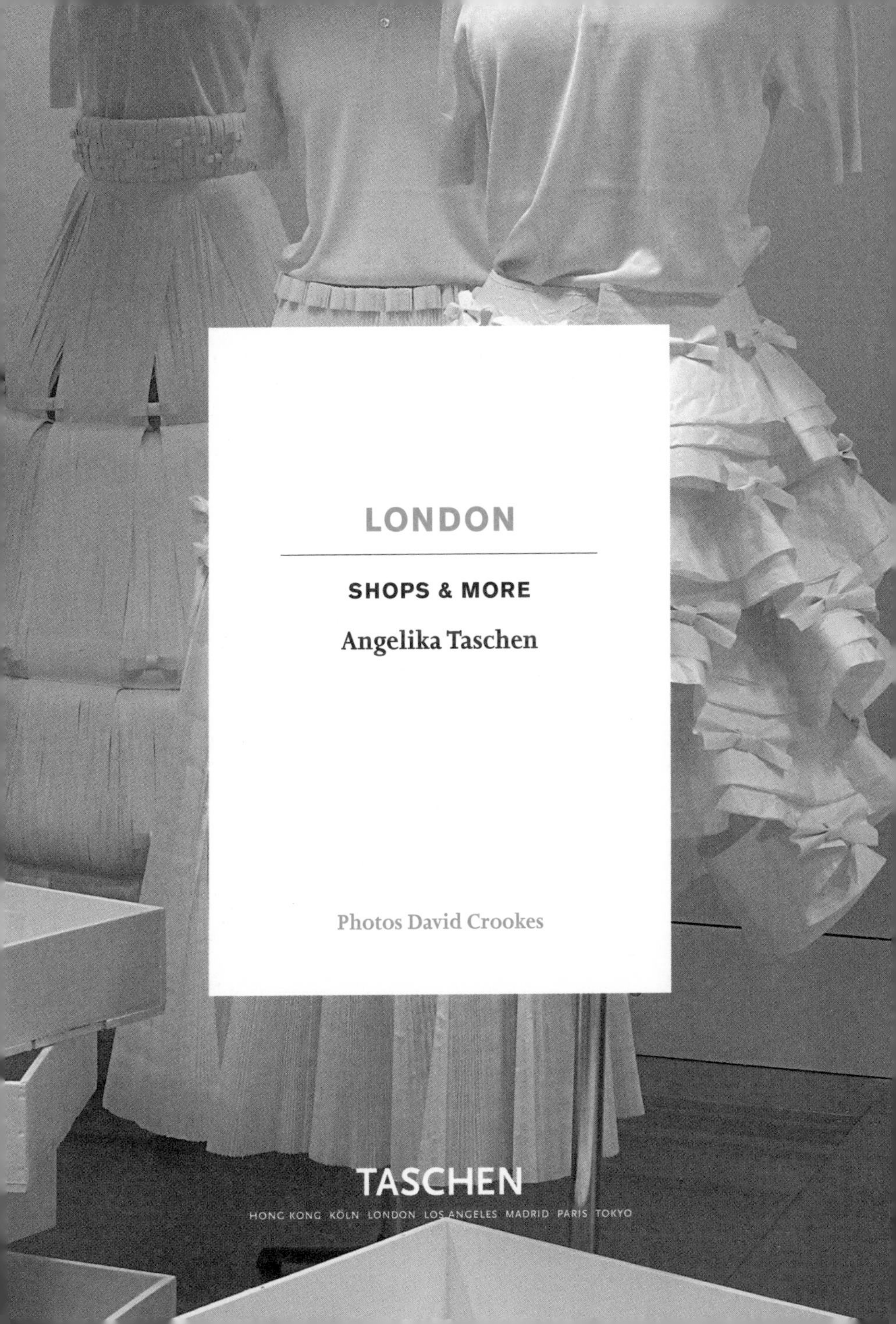

LONDON

SHOPS & MORE

Angelika Taschen

Photos David Crookes

TASCHEN

HONG KONG KÖLN LONDON LOS ANGELES MADRID PARIS TOKYO

James Purdey & Sons

Audley House
57–58 South Audley Street, London W1K 2ED
☎ +44 20 7499 1801
www.purdey.co.uk
Tube: Hyde Park Corner/Green Park

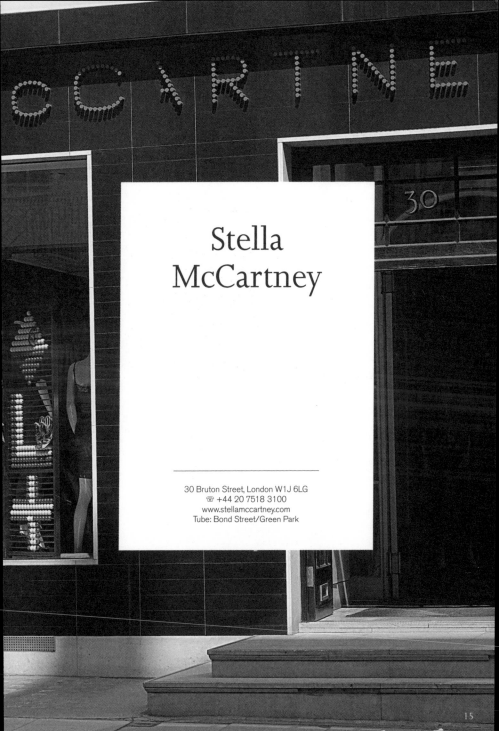

Stella McCartney

30 Bruton Street, London W1J 6LG
☎ +44 20 7518 3100
www.stellamccartney.com
Tube: Bond Street/Green Park

17

Holland
& Holland

31–33 Bruton Street, London W1J 6HH
☎ +44 20 7499 4411
www.hollandandholland.com
Tube: Bond Street/Green Park

Matthew Williamson

---

28 Bruton Street, London W1J 6QH
☏ +44 20 7629 6200
www.matthewwilliamson.com
Tube: Bond Street/Green Park

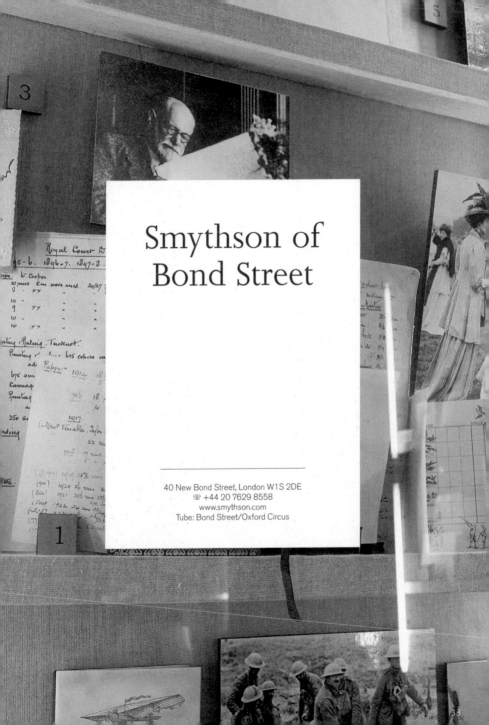

Smythson of Bond Street

40 New Bond Street, London W1S 2DE
☎ +44 20 7629 8558
www.smythson.com
Tube: Bond Street/Oxford Circus

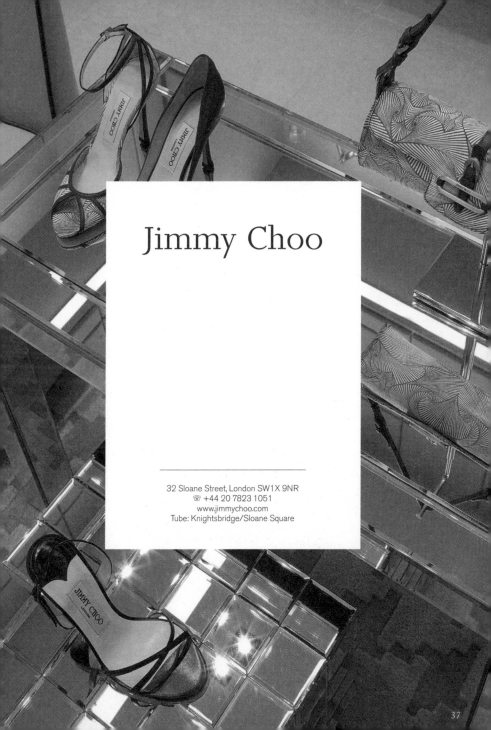

Jimmy Choo

32 Sloane Street, London SW1X 9NR
☎ +44 20 7823 1051
www.jimmychoo.com
Tube: Knightsbridge/Sloane Square

James Purdey & Sons

Audley House
57–58 South Audley Street
London W1K 2ED
☎ +44 20 7499 1801
www.purdey.co.uk

pp. 8/9

Hunting Fashion & Handcrafted Guns
Interior: Very British

Open: Mon–Fri 9.30am–5.30pm, Sat 10am–5pm |
X-Factor: The safari fashion.
This family company has been manufacturing firearms since 1814 – even for the Royals. They also supply the associated tweeds, cashmere pullovers and rubber boots.

Öffnungszeiten: Mo–Fr 9.30–17.30, Sa 10–17 Uhr |
X-Faktor: Die Safari-Mode.
Seit 1814 stellt dieser Familienbetrieb Gewehre her – sogar für die Royals. Dazu gibt's passende Tweedkleidung, Kaschmirpullover und Gummistiefel.

Horaires d'ouverture : Lun–Ven 9h30–17h30, Sam 10h–17h | **Le « petit plus » :** La mode safari. | Depuis 1814, cette entreprise familiale fabrique des armes, même pour le compte de la famille royale. Propose également des vêtements en tweed, des pulls en cachemire et des bottes en caoutchouc.

Stella McCartney

30 Bruton Street
London W1J 6LG
☎ +44 20 7518 3100
www.stellamccartney.com

pp. 14/15

Stylish Designer Fashion
Design: Universal Design Studio

Open: Mon–Sat 10am–6pm, Thur till 7pm | **X-Factor:** The (non-leather!) bags and shoes.
The cool yet feminine fashion is pure London style. The outstandingly tailored ladies' suits are a perfect fit and the chiffon dresses in their bright shades are just wonderful.

Öffnungszeiten: Mo–Sa 10–18, Do bis 19 Uhr | **X-Faktor:** Die Taschen und Schuhe (ohne Leder!) | Die coole und zugleich feminine Mode ist purer London-Style. Besonders gut sitzen die hervorragend geschnittenen Damenanzüge, und wunderschön sind die Chiffonkleider in hellen Tönen.

Horaires d'ouverture : Lun–Sam 10h–18h, Jeu jusqu'à 19h | **Le « petit plus » :** Les sacs et les chaussures (sans cuir !). Mode cool et féminine dans le plus pur style londonien. Les tailleurs sont merveilleusement bien coupés et les robes en mousseline de tons clairs sont magnifiques.

Holland & Holland

31–33 Bruton Street
London W1J 6HH
☎ +44 20 7499 4411
www.hollandandholland.com

pp. 20/21

Safari- & Country-Style Fashion
Interior: Club style

Open: Mon–Fri 9am–6pm, Sat 10am–5pm | **X-Factor:** The legendary "Paradox" gun.
Not just for hunters – this is also the place for people in search of stylish outdoor fashion and a touch of British colonial history.

Öffnungszeiten: Mo–Fr 9–18, Sa 10–17 Uhr | **X-Faktor:** Das legendäre „Paradox"-Gewehr.
Hier sind nicht nur Jäger richtig, sondern alle, die stilvolle Outdoor-Mode suchen und sich in die britische Kolonialgeschichte zurückversetzen wollen.

Horaires d'ouverture : Lun–Ven 9h–18h, Sam 10h–17h | **Le « petit plus » :** « Paradox », l'arme légendaire.
Une bonne adresse pour les chasseurs, mais aussi pour tous ceux qui cherchent une mode outdoor de bon goût et rêvent de l'époque coloniale.

Matthew Williamson

28 Bruton Street
London W1J 6QH
☎ +44 20 7629 6200
www.matthewwilliamson.com

pp. 26/27

Colourful Designer Fashion
Design: Matthew Williamson

Open: Mon–Sat 10am–6pm | **X-Factor:** Helena Christensen and Sienna Miller are regular customers.
This boutique is like a bird of paradise, writes Suzy Menkes – the interior is as richly colourful as the collection itself.

Öffnungszeiten: Mo–Sa 10–18 Uhr | **X-Faktor:** Helena Christensen and Sienna Miller sind Stammkundinnen.
Diese Boutique gleiche einem Paradiesvogel schrieb Suzy Menkes – das Interieur ist so fantastisch bunt wie die Kollektionen.

Horaires d'ouverture : Lun–Sam 10h–18h | **Le « petit plus » :** Helena Christensen et Sienna Miller sont de fidèles clientes. | Suzy Menkes a écrit que cette boutique ressemblait à un oiseau de paradis, sa décoration intérieure étant aussi colorée que ses collections.

Smythson of Bond Street

40 New Bond Street
London W1S 2DE
☎ +44 20 7629 8558
www.smythson.com

pp. 32/33

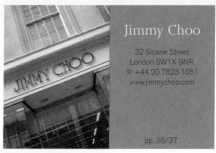

Jimmy Choo

32 Sloane Street
London SW1X 9NR
☎ +44 20 7823 1051
www.jimmychoo.com

pp. 36/37

Sophisticated Leather & Paper Accessories
Interior: Elegant

Open: Mon, Tue, Wed, Fri 9.30am–6pm, Thu 10am–7pm,
Sat 10am–6pm | **X-Factor:** The travel clutch.
In addition to leather goods, Smythson has stylish notebooks
and diaries, as well as writing-paper, which you can have
printed with your personal letterhead.

Öffnungszeiten: Mo, Di, Mi, Fr 9.30–18, Do 10–19, Sa 10–
18 Uhr | **X-Faktor:** Die Travel Clutch.
Neben Lederwaren hat Smythson stilvolle Notiz- und Tage-
bücher sowie Briefpapier im Sortiment, das auf Wunsch
persönlich bedruckt wird.

Horaires d'ouverture : Lun, Mar, Mer, Ven 9h30–18h,
Jeu 10h–19h, Sam 10h–18h | **Le « petit plus » :** Le travel
clutch. Outre la maroquinerie, Smythson propose d'élégants
calepins et agendas ainsi que du papier à lettres imprimé
individuellement.

Glamorous Shoes
Interior: Chic

Open: Mon–Sat 10am–6pm (Wed till 7pm), Sun midday–
5pm | **X-Factor:** The handbags.
Society girl and ex-*Vogue* editor Tamara Mellon is outdoing
the competition – her stilettos are worn by stars like J. Lo
and Scarlett Johanssen.

Öffnungszeiten: Mo–Sa 10–18 (Mi bis 19), So 12–17 Uhr |
X-Faktor: Die Handtaschen.
Society-Girl und Ex-*Vogue*-Redakteurin Tamara Mellon läuft
der Konkurrenz den Rang ab – ihre Stilettos tragen Stars wie
J. Lo und Scarlett Johanssen.

Horaires d'ouverture : Lun–Sam 10h–18h (Mer jusqu'à 19),
Dim 12h–17h | **Le « petit plus » :** Les sacs | Ancienne ré-
dactrice chez *Vogue*, Tamara Mellon est devenue dangereuse
pour ses concurrents – ses chaussures à talons aiguille sont
portées par des stars comme J. Lo et Scarlett Johanssen.

Mayfair
St James's

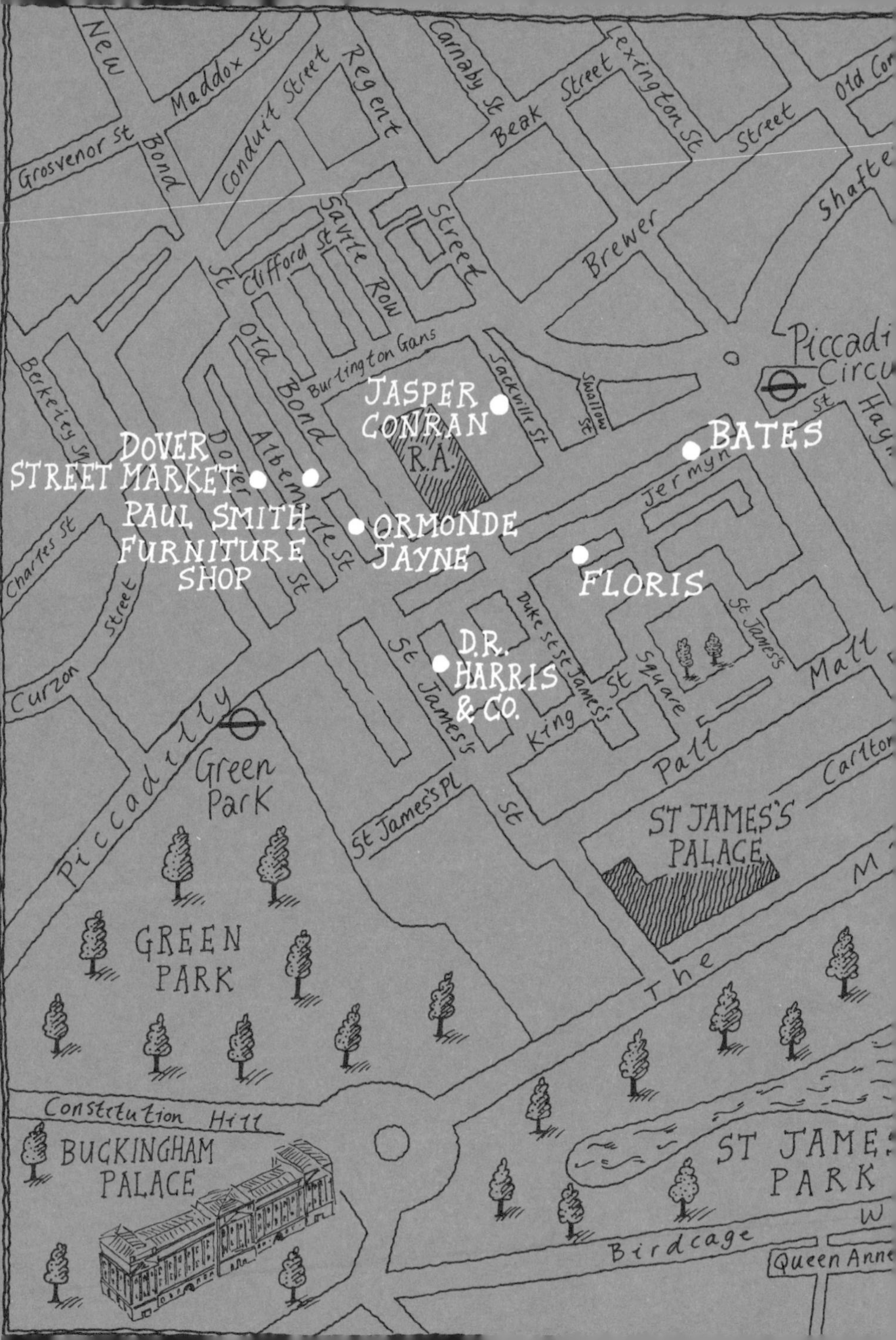
New Bond St
Maddox St
Grosvenor St
Conduit Street
Regent Street
Carnaby St
Beak Street
Lexington St
Old Compton
Shaftesbury
Brewer St
Clifford St
Savile Row
Burlington Gans
Old Bond St
Sackville St
Swallow St
Piccadilly Circus
JASPER CONRAN
R.A.
BATES
Berkeley Sq
DOVER STREET MARKET
Dover St
Albemarle St
PAUL SMITH FURNITURE SHOP
ORMONDE JAYNE
Jermyn St
Haymarket
FLORIS
Charles St
Curzon Street
Duke St St James's
St James's Square
D.R. HARRIS & CO.
St James's St
King St
Pall Mall
Carlton
Piccadilly
Green Park
St James's Pl
ST JAMES'S PALACE
GREEN PARK
The Mall
Constitution Hill
BUCKINGHAM PALACE
ST JAMES'S PARK
Birdcage Walk
Queen Anne

Avenue
Charing Cross Road
Leicester Square
Long Acre
Covent Garden
COVENT GARDEN
Wellington St
Aldwych
PENHALIGON'S
St Martin's Lane
New Row
Bedford St
Maiden Lane
Strand
Cranbourn St
William IV St
John Adam St
Savoy Pl
Embankment
Waterloo Bridge
NATIONAL GALLERY
Trafalgar Square
Charing Cross
Villiers St
Embankment
Cockspur St
Terrace
Northumberland Ave
Hungerford Bridge
Hungerford Footbridges
ROYAL FESTIVAL HALL
Whitehall Place
Whitehall Court
Whitehall
Horse Guards Road
Horseguards Ave
Victoria
R. THAMES
LONDON EYE
Belvedere Road
Downing Street
Parliament St
York Road
Westminster
Gt George St
Parliament Square
Westminster Bridge
HOUSES OF PARLIAMENT
© MICHAELA HILL

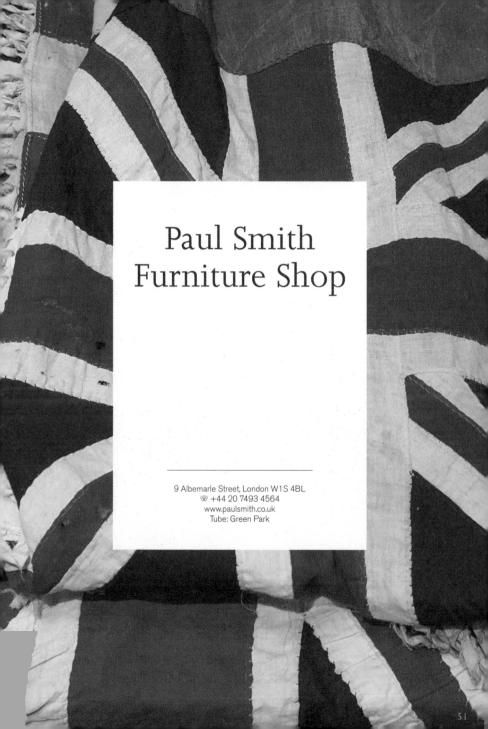

Paul Smith
Furniture Shop

9 Albemarle Street, London W1S 4BL
☎ +44 20 7493 4564
www.paulsmith.co.uk
Tube: Green Park

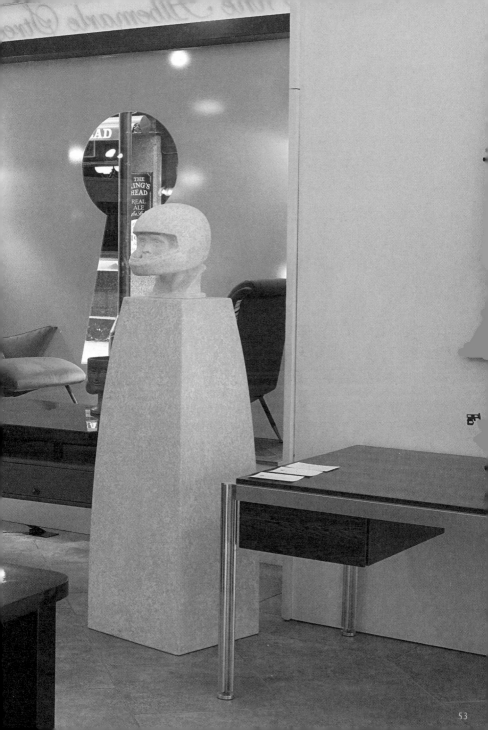

DOVER STREET MARKET

...ME des GARÇONS*

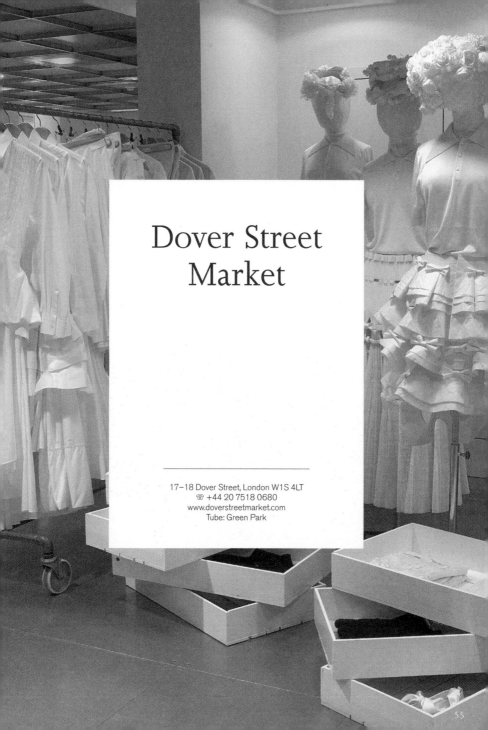

Dover Street Market

17–18 Dover Street, London W1S 4LT
☎ +44 20 7518 0680
www.doverstreetmarket.com
Tube: Green Park

Jasper Conran

36 Sackville Street, London W1S 3EQ
☎ +44 20 7292 9080
www.jasperconran.com
Tube: Piccadilly Circus

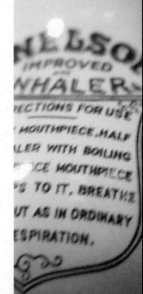

D. R. Harris & Co.

---

29 St James's Street, London SW1A 1HB
☎ +44 20 7930 3915/8753
www.drharris.co.uk
Tube: Green Park

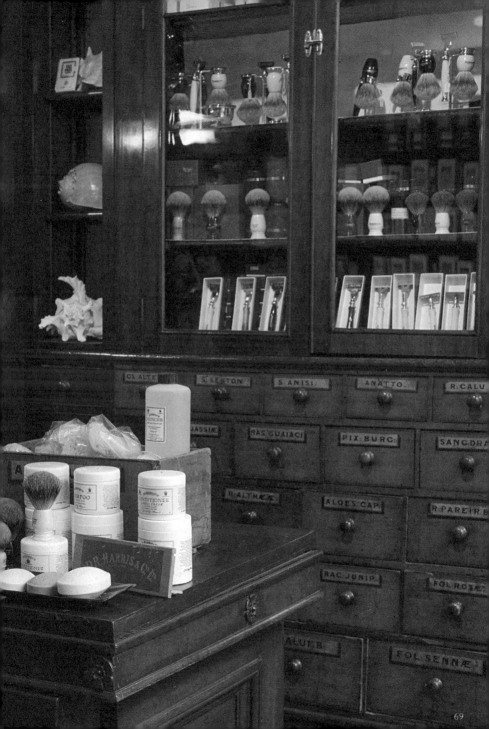

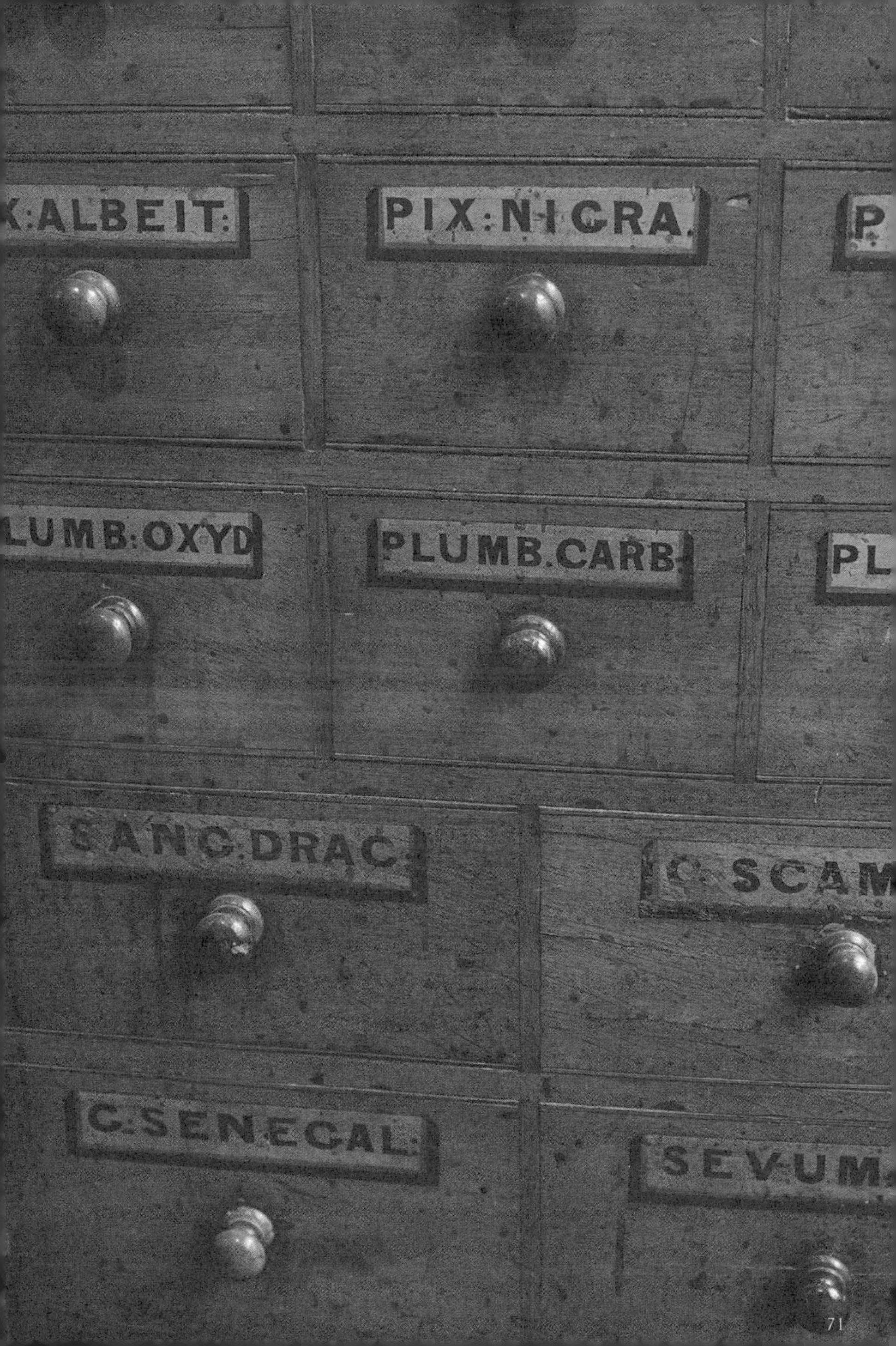

X:ALBEIT:

PIX:NIGRA.

P

LUMB:OXYD

PLUMB.CARB

PL

SANG.DRAC.

C:SCAM

C:SENEGAL.

SEVUM

71

Floris

89 Jermyn Street, London SW1Y 6JH
☎ +44 20 7930 2885
www.florislondon.com
Tube: Green Park/Piccadilly Circus

Bates

21a Jermyn Street, London SW1Y 6HP
☎ +44 20 7734 2722
www.bates-hats.co.uk
Tube: Piccadilly Circus

SMALL HAT BOX
£15.00
LARGE HAT BOX

From
BATES
Gentlemen's Hatter,
Over 100 Years in Jermyn Street,
21ᴬ, JERMYN STREET,
St. James's, London.

Phone:-
020 7734 2722
www.bates-hats.co.uk

From
BATES
Gentlemen's Hatter,
Over 100 Years in Jermyn Street,
21ᴬ, JERMYN STREET,
St. James's, London.

Phone:-
020 7734 2722
www.bates-hats.co.uk

BATES
Gentlemen's Hatter,
Over 100 Years in Jermyn Street,
21ᵃ, JERMYN STREET,
St. James's, London.

Penhaligon's

41 Wellington Street, London WC2E 7BN
☎ +44 20 7836 2150
www.penhaligons.co.uk
Tube: Covent Garden

Ormonde Jayne

The Royal Arcade
28 Old Bond Street
London W1S 4SL
☎ +44 20 7499 1100
www.ormondejayne.com

pp. 46/47

Luxurious Perfumes
Interior: Caulder Moore

Open: Mon–Sat 10am–6pm | **X-Factor:** The perfumed candles.
In a dramatically luxurious atmosphere (gleaming black glass) Linda Pilkington sells exclusive perfumes for which she gets her inspiration on her travels around the world.

Öffnungszeiten: Mo–Sa 10–18 Uhr | **X-Faktor:** Die Duftkerzen.
In luxuriös-dramatischem Ambiente (glänzendes schwarzes Glas) verkauft Linda Pilkington exklusive Düfte. Inspiration findet sie auf ihren Reisen rund um die Welt.

Horaires d'ouverture : Lun–Sam 10h–18h | **Le « petit plus » :** Les bougies odorantes. | Dans une ambiance luxueuse et dramatique (décoration en verre noir brillant) Linda Pilkington vend ses parfums exclusifs. Elle trouve son inspiration au cours de ses voyages autour du monde.

Paul Smith Furniture Shop

9 Albemarle Street
London W1S 4BL
☎ +44 20 7493 4564
www.paulsmith.co.uk

pp. 50/51

Vintage Furniture & Accessories
Interior: Flea-market flair

Open: Mon–Sat 10.30am–6pm | **X-Factor:** The porcelain with the typical Smith bands.
Sir Paul Smith offers an attractive collection of unique furniture from different styles and epochs – a perfect reflection of his British humour!

Öffnungszeiten: Mo–Sa 10.30–18 Uhr | **X-Faktor:** Das Porzellan mit typischen Smith-Streifen.
Sir Paul Smith lockt mit einer einzigartigen Zusammenstellung von Möbeln diverser Stile und Epochen – ein perfektes Spiegelbild seines britischen Humors!

Horaires d'ouverture : Lun–Sam 10h30–18h | **Le « petit plus » :** La porcelaine à rayures typique de chez Smith.
Sir Paul Smith attire ses clients avec un mélange unique en son genre de meubles de styles et d'époques diverses, reflet de son humour anglais !

Dover Street Market

17–18 Dover Street
London W1S 4LT
☎ +44 20 7518 0680
www.doverstreetmarket.com

pp. 54/55

Designer Fashion – presented in Designer Spaces
Design: Alber Elbaz, Duggie Fields, Hiroki Nakamura, et al.

Open: Mon–Sat 11am–6pm, Thu till 7pm | **X-Factor:**
Founded in 2004 by Comme des Garçons.
At DSM stars like Raf Simons and John Galliano, as well as newcomers, show their creations on designer show areas.

Öffnungszeiten: Mo–Sa 11–18, Do bis 19 Uhr | **X-Faktor:**
2004 von Comme des Garçons gegründet.
Bei DSM zeigen Stars wie Raf Simons und John Galliano sowie Newcomer ihre Kreationen auf Designer-Showflächen.

Horaires d'ouverture : Lun–Sam 11h–18h, Jeu jusqu'à 19h | **Le « petit plus » :** Fondé en 2004 par Comme des Garçons | Chez DSM les stars comme Raf Simons et John Galliano, ainsi que les nouveaux venus présentent leurs créations dans des espaces design.

Jasper Conran

36 Sackville Street
London W1S 3EQ
☎ +44 20 7292 9080
www.jasperconran.com

pp. 60/61

Fashion & Luxurious Home Collection
Design: Jasper Conran

Open: Mon–Fri 10.30am–6.30pm, Sat by appointment | **X-Factor:** The private atmosphere.
Along with elegant fashion, this flagship store offers a Home Collection in the modern British style – tasteful and with a touch of Romanticism.

Öffnungszeiten: Mo–Fr 10.30–18.30 Uhr, Sa nach Vereinbarung | **X-Faktor:** Private Atmosphäre.
Neben eleganter Mode bietet der Flagshipstore eine Home Collection im modernen britischen Stil – stilvoll und mit einem Hauch Romantik.

Horaires d'ouverture : Lun–Ven 10h30–18h30, Sam sur rendez-vous | **Le « petit plus » :** L'intimité.
Le flagship store propose une mode élégante, mais aussi une home collection dans le style britannique moderne – chic avec un soupçon de romantisme.

D. R. Harris & Co.

29 St James's Street
London SW1A 1HB
☎ +44 20 7930 3915/8753
www.drharris.co.uk

pp. 66/67

Skincare Products & Perfumes
Interior: Nostalgic pharmacy

Open: Mon–Fri 8.30am–6pm, Sat 9.30am–5pm | **X-Factor:**
Purveyors to His Royal Highness The Prince of Wales.
Founded in 1790, D. R. Harris sells perfumes, creams and
soaps made from old recipes, as well as handmade brushes
and shaving utensils.

Öffnungszeiten: Mo–Fr 8.30–18, Sa 9.30–17 Uhr |
X-Faktor: Hoflieferant des Prinzen von Wales.
1790 gegründet, verkauft D. R. Harris nach alten Rezepten
komponierte Düfte, Cremes und Seifen sowie handgefertigte
Bürsten und Rasierzeug.

Horaires d'ouverture : Lun–Ven 8h30–18h, Sam
9h30–17h | **Le « petit plus » :** Fournisseur du prince de
Galles. | Fondé en 1790, D. R. Harris vend des essences, des
crèmes et des savons préparés d'après d'anciennes recettes,
ainsi que des brosses et des blaireaux fabriqués à la main.

Bates

21a Jermyn Street
London SW1Y 6HP
☎ +44 20 7734 2722
www.bates-hats.co.uk

pp. 76/77

Gentlemen's Hatter
Interior: Rustically British

Open: Mon–Fri 9am–5pm, Sat 9.30am–1pm and 2pm–4pm |
X-Factor: Qualified advice.
Bates has been providing discriminating gentlemen with
made-to-measure top hats, bowlers and tweed caps since
the century before last.

Öffnungszeiten: Mo–Fr 9–17, Sa 9.30–13 und 14–16 Uhr |
X-Faktor: Fachkundige Beratung.
Seit der vorletzten Jahrhundertwende stattet Bates den
eleganten Gentleman mit maßgefertigten Zylindern, Melonen
und Tweedkappen aus.

Horaires d'ouverture : Lun–Ven 9h–17h, Sam 9h30–13h
et 14h–16h | **Le « petit plus » :** Les conseils spécialisés.
Depuis les alentours de 1900, Bates fournit au gentleman
élégant des hauts de forme, des chapeaux melons et des
casquettes en tweed sur mesure.

Floris

89 Jermyn Street
London SW1Y 6JH
☎ +44 20 7930 2885
www.florislondon.com

pp. 72/73

Traditional Scents
Interior: Spanish mahogany

Open: Mon–Fri 9.30am–6pm, Sat 10am–6pm | **X-Factor:**
The velvet tray for your small change.
In 1730 Juan Famenias Floris came to England from Minorca
and opened a hairdressing salon – which became a perfume
empire.

Öffnungszeiten: Mo–Fr 9.30–18, Sa 10–18 Uhr |
X-Faktor: Das Samttablett fürs Wechselgeld.
1730 kam Juan Famenias Floris aus Menorca nach England
und eröffnete einen Friseurladen – daraus ist ein Duftimpe-
rium geworden.

Horaires d'ouverture : Lun–Ven 9h30–18h, Sam
10h–18h | **Le « petit plus » :** Le plateau en argent pour la
monnaie. | En 1730 Juan Famenias Floris quitta Minorque
pour l'Angleterre où il ouvrit un salon de coiffure devenu
aujourd'hui un empire du parfum.

Penhaligon's

41 Wellington Street
London WC2E 7BN
☎ +44 20 7836 2150
www.penhaligons.co.uk

pp. 82/83

Authentic British Scents
Interior: Nostalgic

Open: Mon–Sat 10am–6pm (Thu till 7pm), Sun 12 noon–
6pm | **X-Factor:** Pretty bottles.
From the first creation "Hammam Bouquet" (1872) to Kate
Moss' favourite, "Bluebell": Penhaligon's has British perfume
at its best.

Öffnungszeiten: Mo–Sa 10–18 (Do bis 19), So 12–18 Uhr |
X-Faktor: Hübsche Flakons.
Von der ersten Kreation „Hammam Bouquet" (1872) bis zu
Kate Moss' Lieblingsduft „Bluebell": Penhaligon's bietet
britisches Parfum *at its best*.

Horaires d'ouverture : Lun–Sam 10h–18h (Jeu jusqu'à
19h), Dim 12h–18h | **Le « petit plus » :** Les jolis flacons.
Du « Hammam Bouquet », la toute première création (1872),
à « Bluebell », le parfum favori de Kate Moss, Penhaligon's
propose ce qu'il y a de mieux en parfum britannique.

Soho
Covent Garden
Fitzrovia

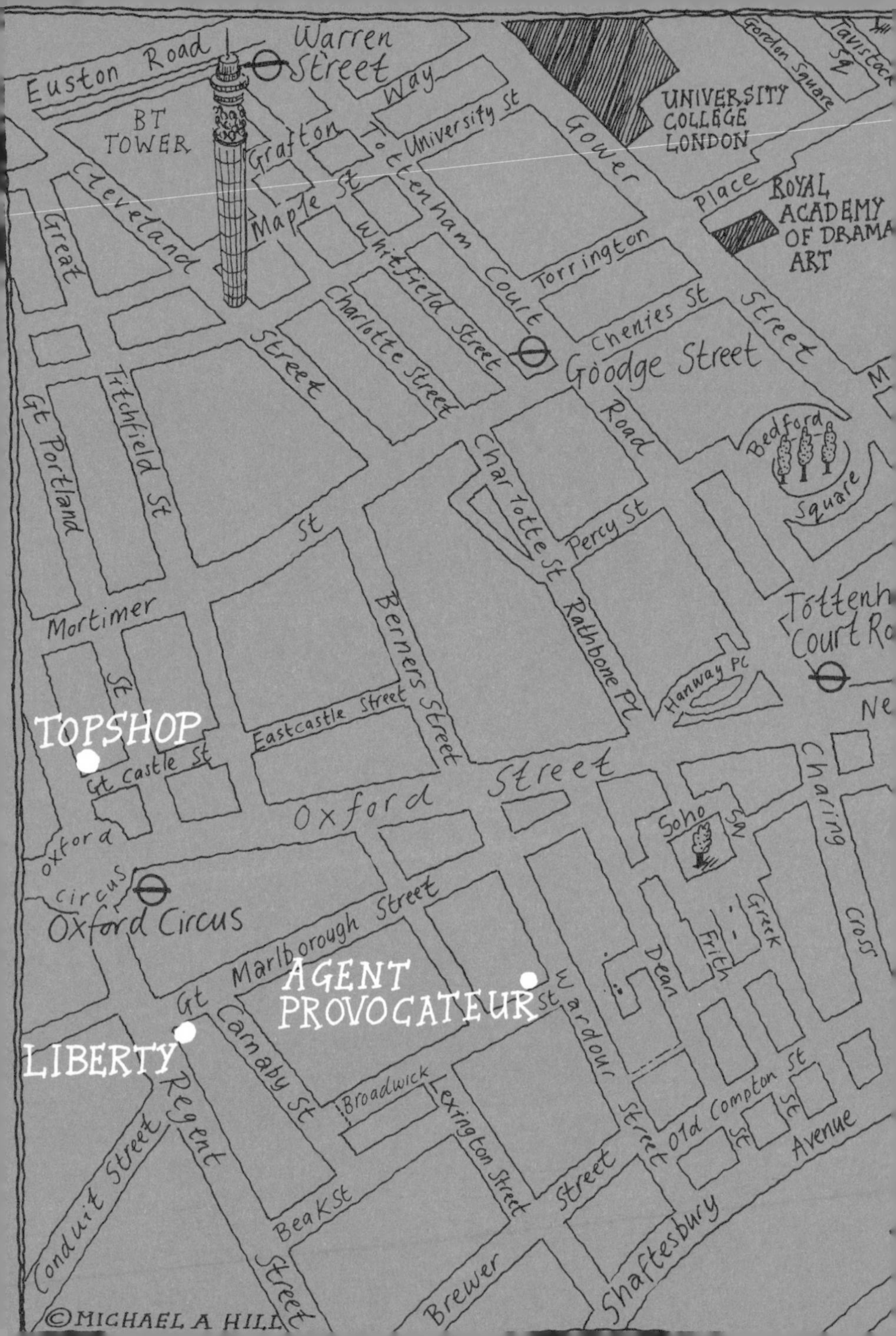
Euston Road
Warren Street
BT TOWER
Grafton Way
Tottenham Court Road
University St
Gordon Square
Tavistock Sq
UNIVERSITY COLLEGE LONDON
Gower Street
Place
ROYAL ACADEMY OF DRAMA ART
Torrington Place
Maple St
Whitfield Street
Charlotte Street
Cleveland Street
Great Portland Street
Chenies St
Goodge Street
Bedford Square
Titchfield St
Gt Portland St
Percy St
Rathbone Pl
Tottenh Court Rd
Hanway Pl
Mortimer St
Berners Street
Eastcastle Street
TOPSHOP
Gt Castle St
Oxford Street
Charing Cross
Soho Sq
Oxford Circus
Great Marlborough Street
AGENT PROVOCATEUR
LIBERTY
Carnaby St
Wardour Street
Dean St
Frith St
Greek St
Broadwick St
Lexington Street
Old Compton St
Regent Street
Conduit Street
Beak St
Brewer Street
Shaftesbury Avenue
©MICHAEL A HILL

CORAM'S FIELDS

Woburn Place

Russell Way

Russell

Bernard Street

Russell Square

Guilford Street

Gt Ormond St

Lamb's Conduit St

Doughty St

Gray's

Northington St

Rosebery Ave

Inn Road

Square

Place

Southampton Row

Old Gloucester St

Boswell St

THE BRITISH MUSEUM

Theobald's Road

Red Lion Street

Bedford Row

Jockey's Fields

Chancery Lane

Great Russell Street

Bloomsbury Way

Procter Street

High Holborn

Chancery Lane

THE LONDON SILVER VAULTS

ford St

MES SMITH & SONS

High Holborn

Holborn

Ave

Macklin St

Parker St

St Queen St

Kingsway

Lincoln's Inn Field

Endell

Neal

Portugal Street

NEAL'S YARD REMEDIES
NEAL'S YARD DAIRY

Drury Lane

ST-MARY LE-STRAND

esbury St

Neal Street

Acre

Bow Street

Aldwych

St St

Covent Garden

Long

Floral

Kings St

Strand

Monmouth

Garrick St

COVENT GARDEN MARKET

COURTAULD INSTITUTE OF ART

Temple

cester yare

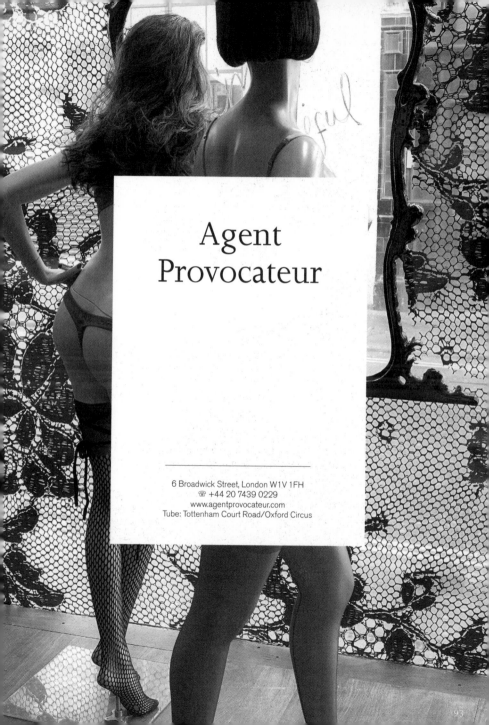

Agent
Provocateur

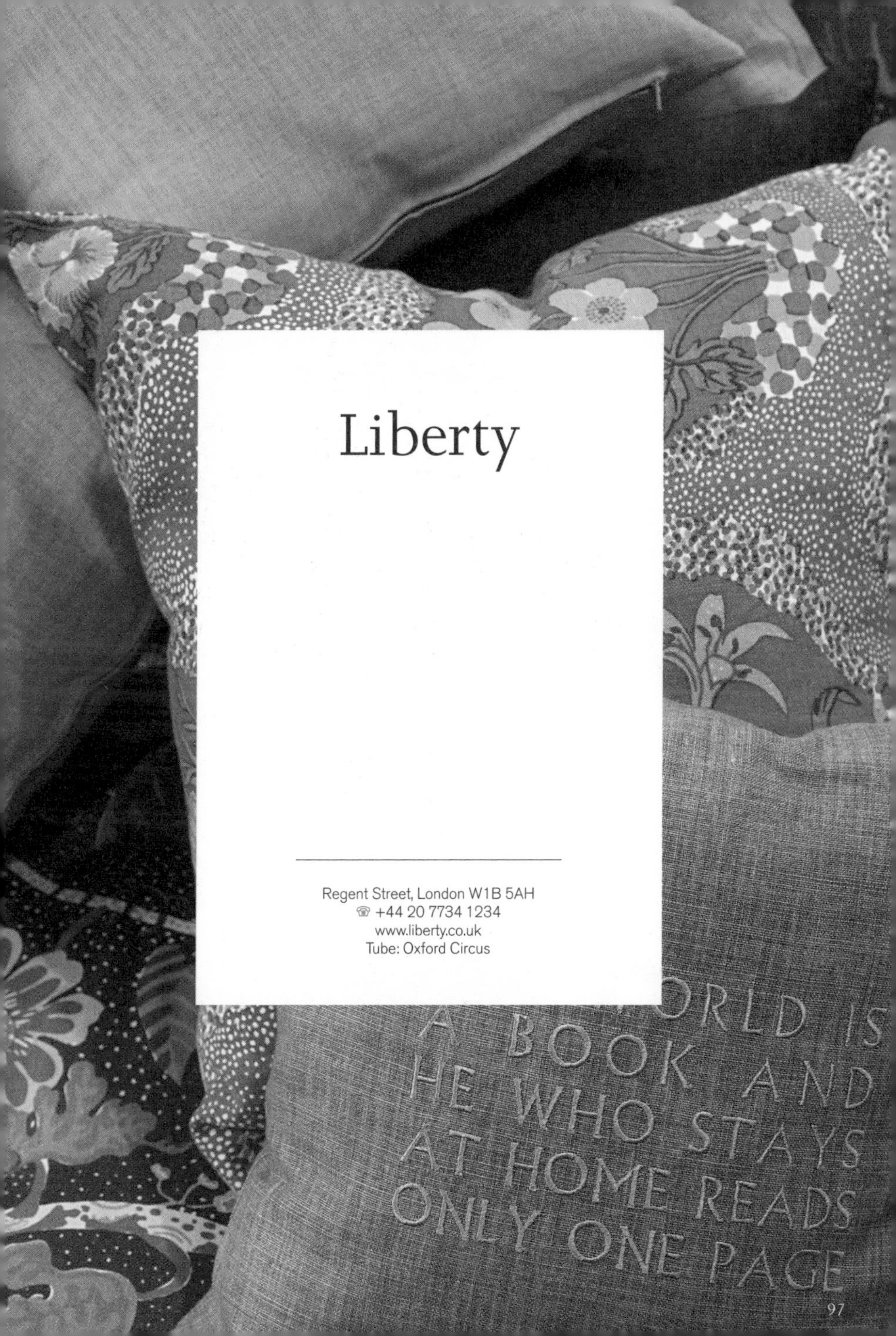

Liberty

Regent Street, London W1B 5AH
☎ +44 20 7734 1234
www.liberty.co.uk
Tube: Oxford Circus

Topshop

36–38 Great Castle Street, London W1W 8L6
☎ +44 20 7636 7700
www.topshop.co.uk
Tube: Oxford Circus

Neal's Yard Remedies

15 Neal's Yard, London WC2H 9DH
☎ +44 20 7379 7222
www.nealsyardremedies.com
Tube: Covent Garden

What goes onto
your skin goes
into your body.

This is why we take such care
to make our UK care products
completely natural - so you
can be healthy as well as
look healthy.

Neal's Yard Dairy

17 Shorts Gardens, London WC2H 9UP
☎ +44 20 7240 5700
www.nealsyarddairy.co.uk
Tube: Covent Garden

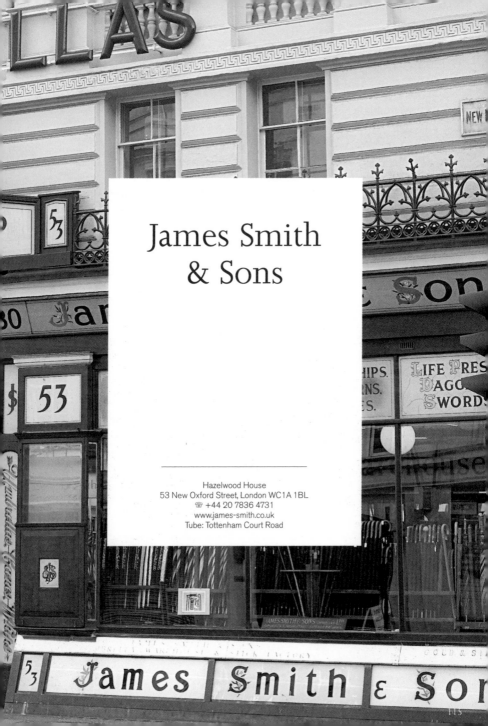

James Smith
& Sons

Hazelwood House
53 New Oxford Street, London WC1A 1BL
☎ +44 20 7836 4731
www.james-smith.co.uk
Tube: Tottenham Court Road

The London Silver Vaults

Chancery House
53–64 Chancery Lane, London WC2A 1QS
☎ +44 20 7242 3844
www.thesilvervaults.com
Tube: Chancery Lane

Agent Provocateur

6 Broadwick Street
London W1V 1FH
☎ +44 20 7439 0229
www.agentprovocateur.com

pp. 92/93

Erotic Lingerie
Interior: Boudoir style

Open: Mon–Wed, Fri/Sat 11am–7pm, Thu 11am–8pm,
Sun midday–5pm | **X-Factor:** The shop assistants' pink
nurselook | In their first shop (1994) Joseph Corre and
Serena Rees tempt customers with provocative underwear
designed with a touch of irony.

Öffnungszeiten: Mo–Mi, Fr/Sa 11–19, Do 11–20, So 12–
17 Uhr | **X-Faktor:** Der rosa Krankenschwester-Look der
Verkäuferinnen.
In ihrem ersten Shop (1994) verführen Joseph Corre und
Serena Rees mit provokant-ironisch designten Dessous.

Horaires d'ouverture : Lun–Mer, Ven/Sam 11h–19h, Jeu
11h–20h, Dim 12h–17h | **Le « petit plus » :** Le look d'infir-
mière des vendeuses en de rose. | Dans leur première bou-
tique (1994) Joseph Corre et Serena Rees vous séduiront
avec des dessous à la fois provocants et ironiques.

Topshop

36–38 Great Castle Street
London W1W 8L6
☎ +44 20 7636 7700
www.topshop.co.uk

pp. 102/103

All About Fashion
Interior: Mega fashion store

Open: Mon–Sat 9am–8pm, Sun midday –6pm | **X-Factor:**
The fashionable maternity wear.
This Topshop flagship store sells catwalk fashion at affordable
prices and has personal-style advisers who bring all the
models to the changing room for you.

Öffnungszeiten: Mo–Sa 9–20, So 12–18 Uhr | **X-Faktor:**
Die schicke Umstandsmode.
Im Topshop-Flagshipstore gibt es Laufsteg-Mode zu
erschwinglichen Preisen – und persönliche Stil-Berater,
die alle Modelle in die Kabine bringen.

Horaires d'ouverture : Lun–Sam 9–20, Dim 12h–18h |
Le « petit plus » : La mode chic pour les futures mamans.
Mode de grands couturiers à des prix abordables et conseils
stylistiques individuels de la part de vendeurs qui vont porter
eux-mêmes tous les modèles dans la cabine d'essayage.

Liberty

Regent Street
London W1B 5AH
☎ +44 20 7734 1234
www.liberty.co.uk

pp. 96/97

Legendary Destination Store in a Tudor-Style Building
Interior: Stairs and galleries made from the wood of the last
British warships

Open: Mon–Wed, Fri 10am–8pm (Thu till 9pm), Sat midday–
7pm (Sun till 6pm) | **X-Factor:** The interiors section.
Behind its historical façade Liberty has altogether smart
fashion plus vintage and designer furniture.

Öffnungszeiten: Mo–Mi/Fr 10–20 (Do bis 21), Sa 12–
19 Uhr (So bis 18) | **X-Faktor:** Die Interior-Abteilung.
Hinter seiner historischen Fassade bietet Liberty todschicke
Mode, Vintage- und Design-Möbel.

Horaires d'ouverture : Lun–Mer/Ven 10h–20h (Jeu jusqu'à
21h), Sam 12h–19h (Dim jusqu'à 18h) | **Le « petit plus » :**
Le rayon décoration intérieure.
Derrière sa façade historique, Liberty propose une mode
terriblement chic ainsi que des meubles vintage et design.

Neal's Yard Remedies

15 Neal's Yard
London WC2H 9DH
☎ +44 20 7379 7222
www.nealsyardremedies.com

pp. 106/107

Organic Skin & Body Care
Interior: Friendly

Open: Mon–Fri 10.30am–7pm, Sat 9.30am–7pm, Sun
11am–6pm | **X-Factor:** The "Therapy Rooms" (2 Neal's Yard).
Natural cosmetics and remedies are sold in cobalt blue
bottles or complete with blue labels.

Öffnungszeiten: Mo–Fr 10.30–19, Sa 9.30–19, So 11–
18 Uhr | **X-Faktor:** Die „Therapy Rooms" (2 Neal's Yard).
In kobaltblaue Fläschchen gefüllt oder mit blauen Etiketten
versehen, werden Naturkosmetik und Bio-Heilmittel ange-
boten.

Horaires d'ouverture : Lun–Ven 10h30–19h, Sam 9h30–
19h, Dim 11h–18h | **Le « petit plus » :** Les « Therapy
Rooms » (2 Neal's Yard). | Les produits cosmétiques naturels
et les préparations bios sont présentés dans de petites bou-
teilles bleu cobalt ou munies d'étiquettes bleues.

Neal's Yard Dairy

17 Shorts Gardens
London WC2H 9UP
☎ +44 20 7240 5700
www.nealsyarddairy.co.uk

pp. 110/111

Delicious Farm Cheese
Interior: Country style

Open: Mon–Thu 11am–6.30pm, Fri/Sat 10am–6.30pm |
X-Factor: The "stinking bishop" from Gloucestershire.
A land of milk and honey for people who love British
cheeses – the aromatic sorts are made by independent
regional farmers.

Öffnungszeiten: Mo–Do 11–18.30, Fr/Sa 10–18.30 Uhr |
X-Faktor: Der „stinking bishop" aus Gloucestershire.
Ein Schlaraffenland für alle, die britischen Käse lieben – die
duftenden Sorten stammen von unabhängigen regionalen
Farmern.

Horaires d'ouverture : Lun–Jeu 11h–18h30, Ven/Sam
10h–18h30 | **Le « petit plus » :** Le « stinking bishop » de
Gloucestershire. | Un pays de cocagne pour tous ceux qui
aiment le fromage anglais – les variétés odorantes sont
fabriquées par des fermiers régionaux indépendants.

The London Silver Vaults

Chancery House
53–64 Chancery Lane
London WC2A 1QS
☎ +44 20 7242 3844
www.thesilvervaults.com

pp. 118/119

Fine Antique Silver Ware
Interior: Treasure vault

Open: Mon–Fri 9am–5.30pm, Sat till 1pm | **X-Factor:** Like
a journey into the past.
English silver is regarded as the finest in the world – 37
shops offer pieces from all epochs in the vaults of Chancery
House.

Öffnungszeiten: Mo–Fr 9–17.30, Sa bis 13 Uhr | **X-Faktor:**
Wie eine Reise in die Vergangenheit.
Englisches Silber gilt als das feinste der Welt – in den
Gewölben des Chancery House wird in 37 Shops mit Stücken
aller Epochen gehandelt.

Horaires d'ouverture : Lun–Ven 9h–17h30, Sam jusqu'à
13h | **Le « petit plus » :** Un voyage dans le temps.
L'argenterie anglaise est réputée comme étant la plus fine
au monde – dans les salles voûtées de la Chancery House,
37 boutiques vendent des pièces datant de toutes les époques.

James Smith & Sons

Hazelwood House
53 New Oxford Street
London WC1A 1BL
☎ +44 20 7836 4731
www.james-smith.co.uk

pp. 114/115

Authentic British Umbrellas
Interior: Victorian

Open: Mon–Fri 9.30am–5.15pm, Sat from 10am | **X-Factor:**
The parasols – for when the rain stops.
A classic shop that simply has to be seen: both standard
umbrellas and designer models, as well as walking sticks.

Öffnungszeiten: Mo–Fr 9.30–17.15, Sa ab 10 Uhr |
X-Faktor: Die Sonnenschirme – falls es mal nicht regnet.
Ein Klassiker, den man gesehen haben sollte: Neben altbe-
währten Regenschirmen gibt es auch Designmodelle und
Gehstöcke.

Horaires d'ouverture : Lun–Ven 9h30–17h15, Sam à
partir de 10h | **Le « petit plus » :** Les ombrelles, pour les
jours sans pluie.
Un must quand on visite Londres : à côté des parapluies
traditionnels, on y trouve des modèles design et des cannes.

REGENT'S PARK

Park Road

Outer Circle

Regent's Park

Regent's Park Crs

Gloucester

Baker Street

Baker Street

Marylebone Road

High Street

Devonshire Pl

Harley Street

Devonshire

● DAUNT BOOKS

Paddington St

MARYLEBONE FARMERS' MARKET

Moxton St

Cramer St

Marylebone

New Cavendish St

Montagu Pl

Dorset St

Blandford

Street

George Street

Thayer St

Marylebone

Wimpole Street

Bryanston Sq

Montagu Square

Place

Manchester Square

COURTAULD INST.

Portman

Street

George St

Portman Square

Wigmore

THE BUTTON QUEEN

Street

Henrietta

Upper Berkeley

St

Square

Seymour

Marble Arch

Portman St

Oxford Street

Bond Street

So Molton

Davies St

MARBLE ARCH

©MICHAELA HILA

Marylebone

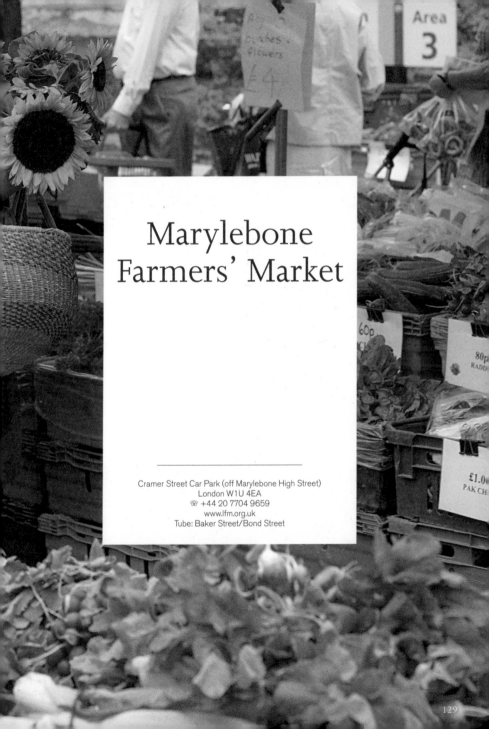

Marylebone Farmers' Market

Cramer Street Car Park (off Marylebone High Street)
London W1U 4EA
☎ +44 20 7704 9659
www.lfm.org.uk
Tube: Baker Street/Bond Street

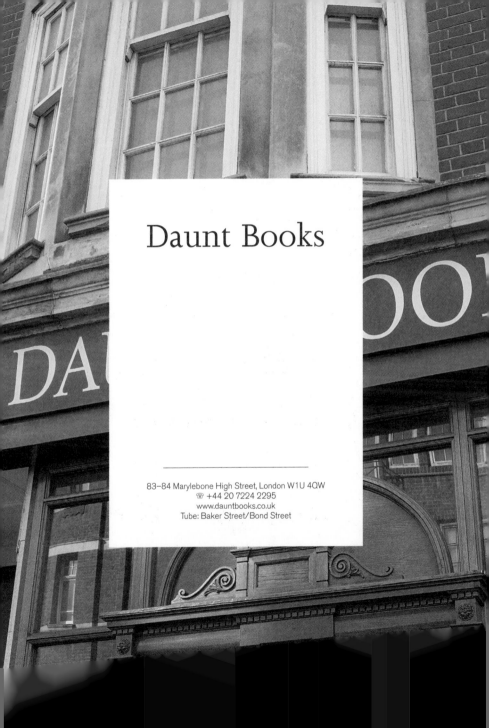

Daunt Books

83–84 Marylebone High Street, London W1U 4QW
☏ +44 20 7224 2295
www.dauntbooks.co.uk
Tube: Baker Street/Bond Street

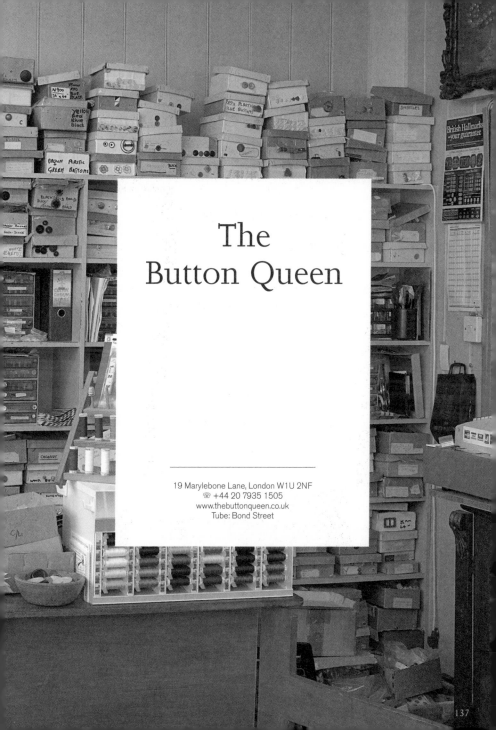

The
Button Queen

19 Marylebone Lane, London W1U 2NF
☏ +44 20 7935 1505
www.thebuttonqueen.co.uk
Tube: Bond Street

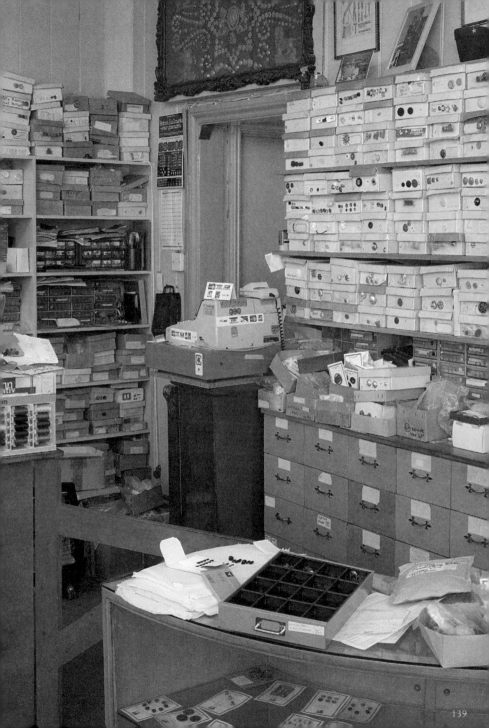

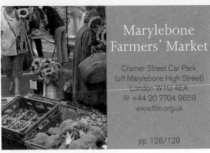

Marylebone Farmers' Market

Cramer Street Car Park
(off Marylebone High Street)
London W1U 4EA
☏ +44 20 7704 9659
www.lfm.org.uk

pp. 128/129

Daunt Books

83–84 Marylebone
High Street
London W1U 4QW
☏ +44 20 7224 2295
www.dauntbooks.co.uk

pp. 132/133

Atmospheric Farmers' Market
Setting: Outdoors

Open: Sun 10am–2pm | **X-Factor:** Perfect for picnic necessities.
Here British farmers offer fresh products like cheese, free-range eggs, vegetables and bread. This market has turned the quarter into a food Mecca.

Öffnungszeiten: So 10–14 Uhr | **X-Faktor:** Perfekt zur Picknick-Vorbereitung.
Hier bieten britische Bauern frische Ware wie Käse, Freiland-Eier, Gemüse und Brot an. Dieser Markt hat das Viertel zum Food-Mekka gemacht.

Horaires d'ouverture : Dim 10h–14h | **Le « petit plus » :** Parfait pour préparer un pique-nique.
Les fermiers anglais proposent ici leurs produits frais comme le fromage, les œufs fermiers, les légumes et le pain. Ce marché a transformé le quartier en paradis de l'alimentation.

Bookshop in an Edwardian Building
Interior: With oak galleries and skylight

Open: Mon–Sat 9am–7.30pm, Sun 11am–6pm | **X-Factor:** The selection of travel books.
The most beautiful bookshop in London is in a building dating from the time of Edward VII and is exceptionally well stocked.

Öffnungszeiten: Mo–Sa 9–19.30, So 11–18 Uhr | **X-Faktor:** Die Auswahl an Reisetiteln.
Die schönste Buchhandlung Londons ist in einem Gebäude aus der Zeit Eduards VII. untergebracht und fantastisch sortiert.

Horaires d'ouverture : Lun–Sam 9h–19h30, Dim 11h–18h | **Le « petit plus » :** Le grand choix de livres de voyage.
Très bien achalandée, la plus belle librairie de Londres se trouve dans un immeuble construit à l'époque d'Edouard VII.

The Button Queen

19 Marylebone Lane
London W1U 2NF
☏ +44 20 7935 1505
www.thebuttonqueen.co.uk

pp. 136/137

Historic & Modern Buttons
Interior: Stacks and stacks of boxes

Open: Mon–Wed 10am–5pm, Thu/Fri 10am–6pm, Sat 10am–4pm | **X-Factor:** A legend since the 1960s.
The market stall of London's "Queen of Buttons" has become a treasure trove for fashion and costume designers and for collectors.

Öffnungszeiten: Mo–Mi 10–17, Do/Fr 10–18, Sa 10–16 Uhr | **X-Faktor:** Eine Legende seit den 1960ern.
Aus dem Marktstand der „Knopfkönigin" von London wurde eine Fundgrube für Mode- und Kostümdesigner sowie Sammler.

Horaires d'ouverture : Lun–Mer 10h–17h, Jeu/Ven 10h–18h, Sam 10h–16h | **Le « petit plus » :** Légendaire depuis les années 1960. | L'étal de la « reine du bouton » londonienne est devenu une caverne d'Ali Baba pour les grands couturiers, les costumiers et les collectionneurs.

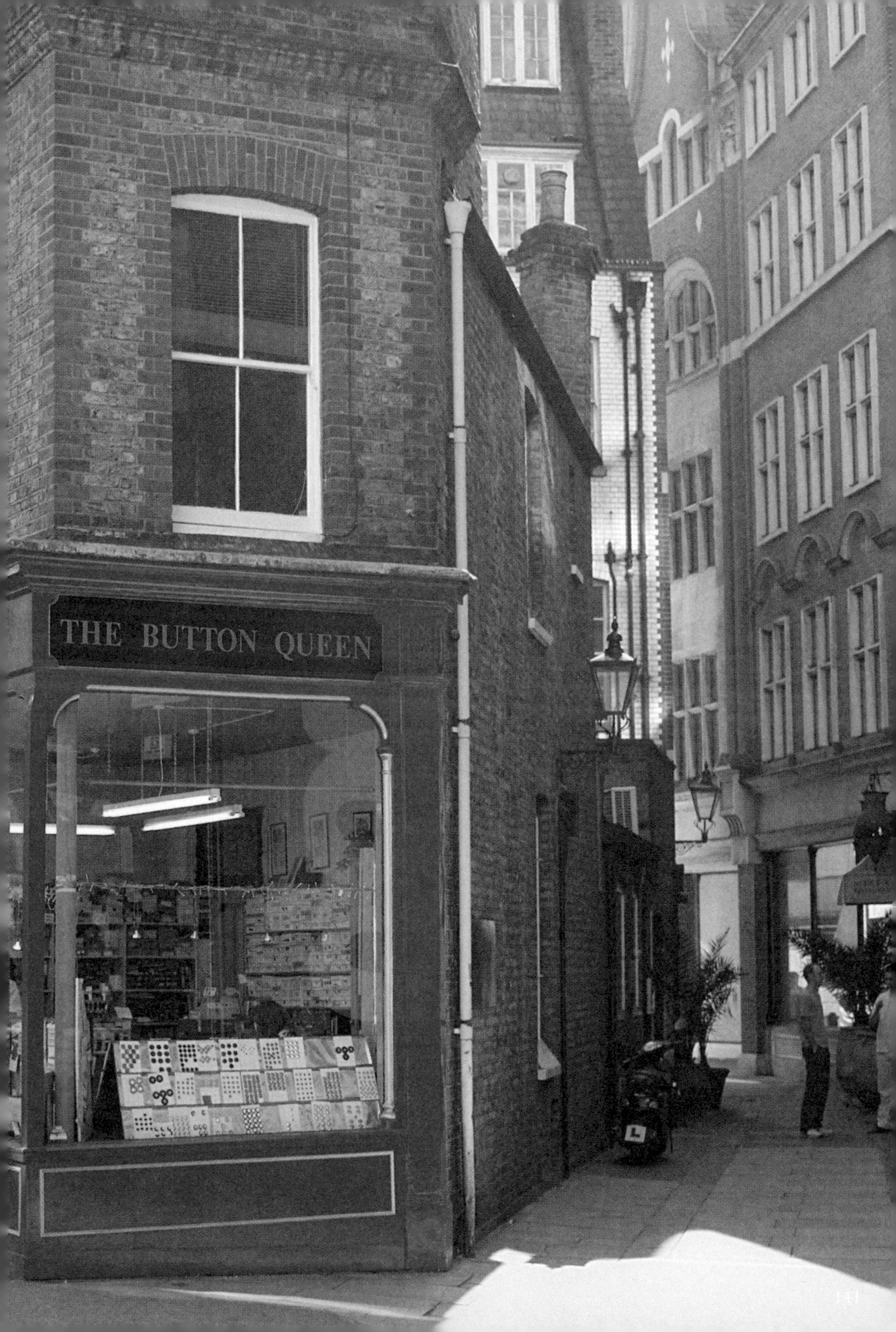
THE BUTTON QUEEN

South Kensington Chelsea

Queen's Gate

Imperial College Road

SCIENCE MUSEUM

NATURAL HISTORY MUSEUM

Exhibition Road

Cromwell Road

VICTORIA & ALBERT MUSEUM

BROMPTON ORATORY

Brompton Square

Cheval Place

Brompton Rd

Beauch

Yeoman's Row

Egerton Terr

Walton

Thurloe Place

Thurloe St

Harrington Rd

Stanhope Gdns

Thurloe St

South Kensington

Brompton Rd

Denyer

Drayco

Sloane

Old Brompton Road

Summer Pl

Onslow Sq

Onslow Gdns

Onslow Gdns

Cranley Gdns

Fulham Road

Old Church Street

Ixworth Place

Elystan St

Cale Street

Sydney Street

Britten St

Dovehouse Street

Jubilee Pl

Markham St

Ki n Rd

Drayton Gdns

FARROW & BALL

Flood Street

Hans Crescent

Hans Rd

Basil St

Hans Place

Pont Place

Pont Street

Sloane Street

Pavilion Road

Pont Street

Lowndes St

Cadogan Place

Cadogan Lane

Chesham St

Lyall St

Eaton Place

King's Road

Eaton

Belgrave Square

Upp Belgrave St

Belgrave Pl

Eaton Square

Elizabeth Street

St George's

JO MALONE

DAVID MELLOR

EMMA HOPE

PHILIP TREACY

Eaton

Sloane Square

Sloane Square

Chester Row

Eaton Terr

Ebury

Cadogan Street

Draycott Place

Cadogan Avenue

Avenue

Sloane Road

Lower Sloane Street

Pimlico Rd

Bloomfield Terrace

Ranelagh Gr

Cheltenham Terrace

St Leonard's Terr

Franklin's Row

Royal Hospital Road

Smith Street

Tedworth Sq

Road

Chelsea Bridge Road

Ebury Bridge Road

ROYAL HOSPITAL CHELSEA

© MICHAELA HILL

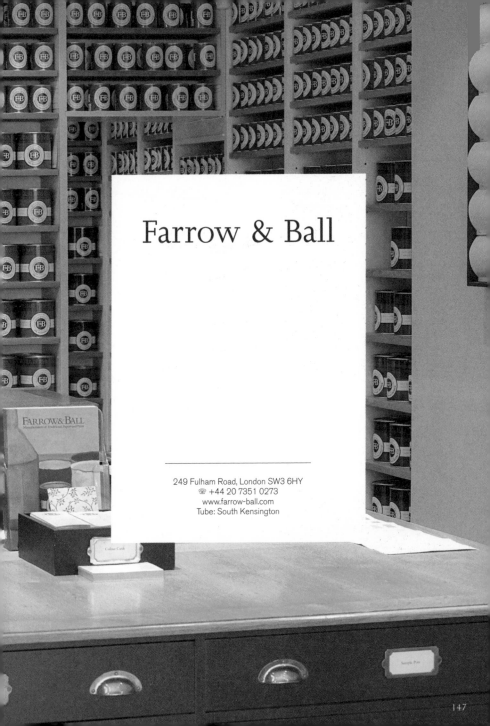

Farrow & Ball

249 Fulham Road, London SW3 6HY
☎ +44 20 7351 0273
www.farrow-ball.com
Tube: South Kensington

FARROW&BAL

Manufacturers of Traditional Papers and Pa

The Ringwold Papers

FARROW

Manufacturers of Tradit

The Gris

Jo Malone

150 Sloane Street, London SW1X 9BX
☎ +44 20 7730 2100
www.jomalone.co.uk
Tube: Sloane Square

153

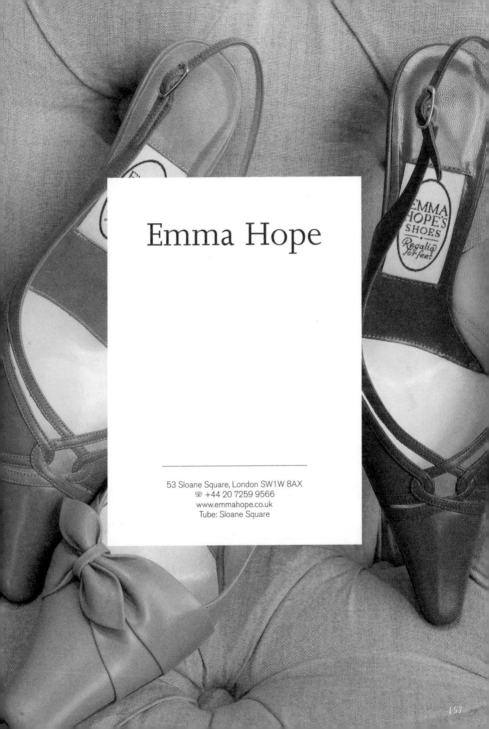

Emma Hope

53 Sloane Square, London SW1W 8AX
☎ +44 20 7259 9566
www.emmahope.co.uk
Tube: Sloane Square

David Mellor

---

4 Sloane Square, London SW1W 8EE
☎ +44 20 7730 4259
www.davidmellordesign.com
Tube: Sloane Square

SAUCEPANS

COOKING POTS

TABLEWARE

MINCERS

SCALES MEASURES

TINS

SIEVES STRAINERS

WOODWARE

KITCHEN GLASS

SPOONS SERVERS

COFFEE MAKERS

CORKSCREWS

KITCHEN LINEN

STAINLESS STEEL

KITCHEN TOOLS

COPPERWARE

COOKERY BOOKS

ICING EQUIPMENT

Philip Treacy

69 Elizabeth Street, London SW1W 9PJ
☎ +44 20 7730 3992
www.philiptreacy.co.uk
Tube: Sloane Square/Victoria

Farrow & Ball

249 Fulham Road
London SW3 6HY
☎ +44 20 7351 0273
www.farrow-ball.com

pp. 146/147

Traditional Paint & Wallpapers
Interior: A cross between a shop and a studio

Open: Mon–Fri 8.30am–5.30pm, Sat 10am–5pm | **X-Factor:**
Personal service.
This manufactory has been producing decorative paints in all
shades since 1930. They also print wallpapers using traditional techniques.

Öffnungszeiten: Mo–Fr 8.30–17.30, Sa 10–17 Uhr |
X-Faktor: Persönlicher Service.
Seit 1930 stellt diese Manufaktur Wandfarben in allen
Nuancen her und bedruckt Tapeten nach traditionellen
Techniken.

Horaires d'ouverture : Lun–Ven 8h30–17h30, Sam 10h–
17h | **Le « petit plus » :** Service individuel.
Depuis 1930 cette manufacture produit des peintures pour
les murs dans toutes les nuances et imprime des papiers
peints selon des techniques traditionnelles.

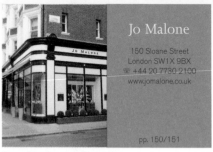

Jo Malone

150 Sloane Street
London SW1X 9BX
☎ +44 20 7730 2100
www.jomalone.co.uk

pp. 150/151

Elegant Perfumes & Cosmetics
Interior: Elegant white and black

Open: Mon, Tue, Sat 9.30am–6pm, Wed–Fri 9.30am–7pm,
Sun 12 noon–5pm | **X-Factor:** The stylish packaging.
Jo Malone's career began with facials – later she expanded
into heavenly perfumes and make-up.

Öffnungszeiten: Mo, Di, Sa 9.30–18, Mi–Fr 9.30–19, So
12–17 Uhr | **X-Faktor:** Die stilvollen Verpackungen.
Jo Malones Karriere begann mit Facials – später erweiterte
sie ihr Angebot um himmlische Düfte und Make-ups.

Horaires d'ouverture : Lun, Mar, Sam 9h30–18h, Mer–Ven
9h30–19h, Dim 12h–17h | **Le « petit plus » :** L'emballage
très chic. | La carrière de Jo Malone a débuté avec les soins
pour le visage auxquels il a ajouté plus tard des parfums et
des produits de maquillage.

Emma Hope

53 Sloane Square
London SW1W 8AX
☎ +44 20 7259 9566
www.emmahope.co.uk

pp. 156/157

Chic Shoes
Interior: Effective

Open: Mon–Sat 10am–6.30pm (Wed till 7pm), Sun mid-
day– 5pm | **X-Factor:** The sneakers.
Emma Hope designs shoes in wonderful colours and with
pert little details – Paul Smith and Anna Sui models wear
them on the catwalk.

Öffnungszeiten: Mo–Sa 10–18.30 (Mi bis 19), So 12–
17 Uhr | **X-Faktor:** Die Sneakers.
Emma Hope entwirft Schuhe in wunderbaren Farben und mit
hübsch-frechen Details – Models von Paul Smith oder Anna
Sui tragen sie auf dem Catwalk.

Horaires d'ouverture : Lun–Sam 10h–18h30 (Mer jusqu'à
19), Dim 12h–17h | **Le « petit plus » :** Les sneakers.
Emma Hope crée des chaussures aux couleurs fantastiques
agrémentées de détails insolents. Les mannequins de Paul
Smith ou de Anna Sui les portent lors des défilés de mode.

David Mellor

4 Sloane Square
London SW1W 8EE
☎ +44 20 7730 4259
www.davidmellordesign.com

pp. 160/161

Designer Kitchenware & Cutlery
Interior: A large professional kitchen

Open: Mon–Sat 9.30am–6pm, Sun 11am–5pm | **X-Factor:**
The legendary "Pride" cutlery.
David Mellor is London's "King of Cutlery" – and also has
other utensils for the perfect kitchen.

Öffnungszeiten: Mo–Sa 9.30–18, So 11–17 Uhr |
X-Faktor: Die legendäre Besteckserie „Pride".
David Mellor ist der „Besteckkönig" von London – und sorgt
auch mit weiteren Utensilien für die perfekte Küchenaus-
stattung.

Horaires d'ouverture : Lun–Sam 9h30–18h, Dim 11h–
17h | **Le « petit plus » :** La légendaire série de couverts
« Pride ». | David Mellor est le « roi des couverts » de Londres,
et avec ses autres ustensiles de cuisine vous serez parfaite-
ment équipé.

Philip Treacy

69 Elizabeth Street
London SW1W 9PJ
☏ +44 20 7730 3992
www.philiptreacy.co.uk

pp. 164/165

Eccentric Hats
Interior: Meier-Scupin & Partner, Munich

Open: By appointment | **X-Factor:** Karl Lagerfeld and
Alexander McQueen place orders here.
As a child Philip Treacy made hats for his sister's dolls. Today
he supplies to designers, models and Ascot visitors, including
Camilla and Kate!

Öffnungszeiten: Nach Vereinbarung | **X-Faktor:** Hier
ordern Karl Lagerfeld und Alexander McQueen.
Als Kind machte Philip Treacy Hüte für die Puppen seiner
Schwester, heute stattet er Designer, Models und die Ascot-
Society aus. Auch Camilla und Kate!

Horaires d'ouverture : Sur rendez-vous | **Le « petit plus » :**
Karl Lagerfeld et Alexander McQueen sont des clients.
Philip Treacy faisait des chapeaux pour les poupées de sa
sœur, aujourd'hui il est le fournisseur des stylistes, des mannequins et de la Ascot-Society. Sans oublier Camilla et Kate !

Notting Hill

ANYA HINDMARCH

MELT

PAUL
SMITH

©MICHAEL A HILL

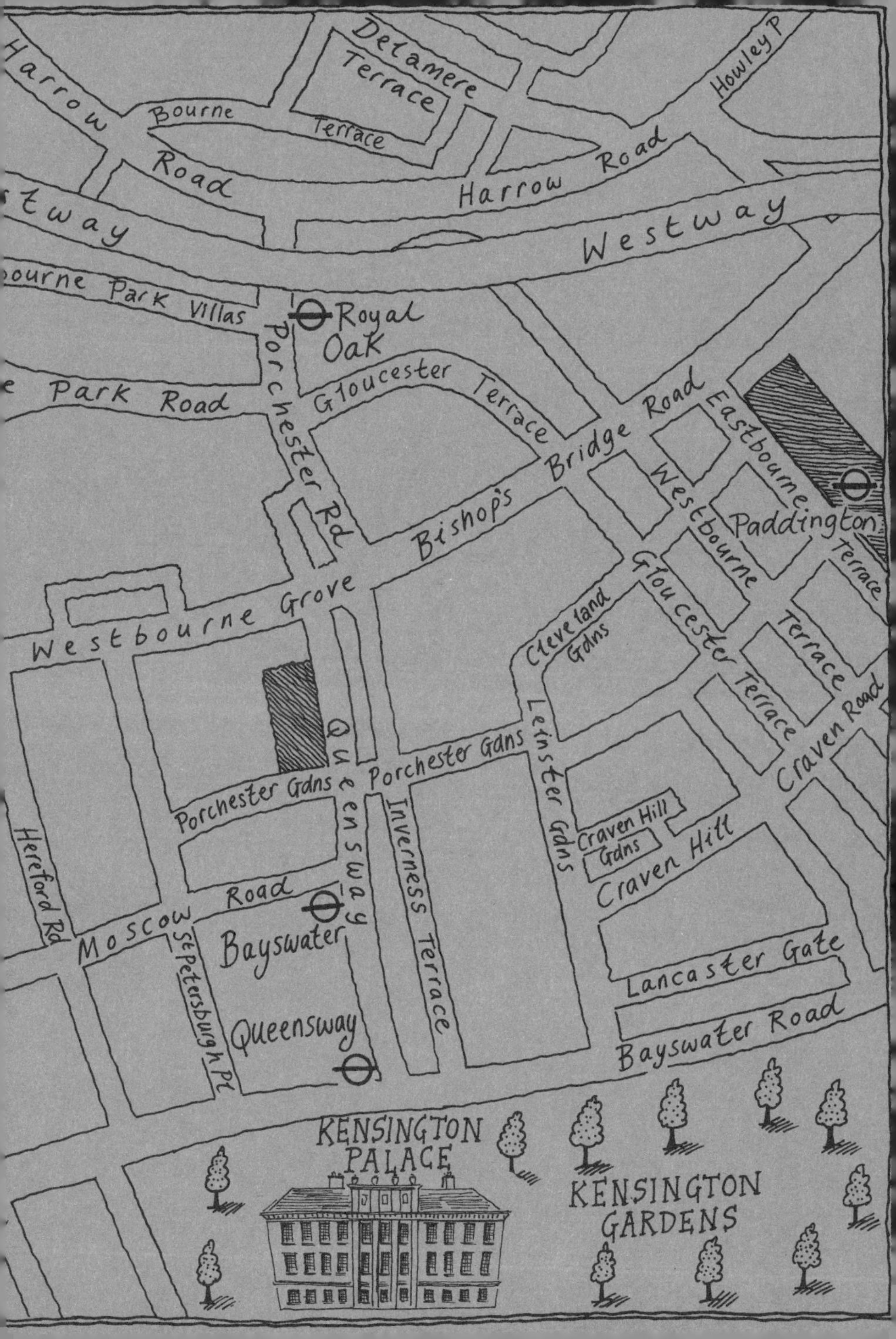

Harrow Road
Delamere Terrace
Bourne Terrace
Howley P
Harrow Road
Westway
Westway
ourne Park Villas
Royal Oak
e Park Road
Porchester Rd
Gloucester Terrace
Bishop's Bridge Road
Eastbourne Terrace
Paddington
Westbourne Grove
Westbourne Terrace
Gloucester Terrace
Cleveland Gdns
Terrace
Craven Road
Queensway
Porchester Gdns
Porchester Gdns
Leinster Gdns
Craven Hill Gdns
Craven Hill
Hereford Rd
Moscow Road
Inverness Terrace
St Petersburgh Pl
Bayswater
Queensway
Lancaster Gate
Bayswater Road
KENSINGTON PALACE
KENSINGTON GARDENS

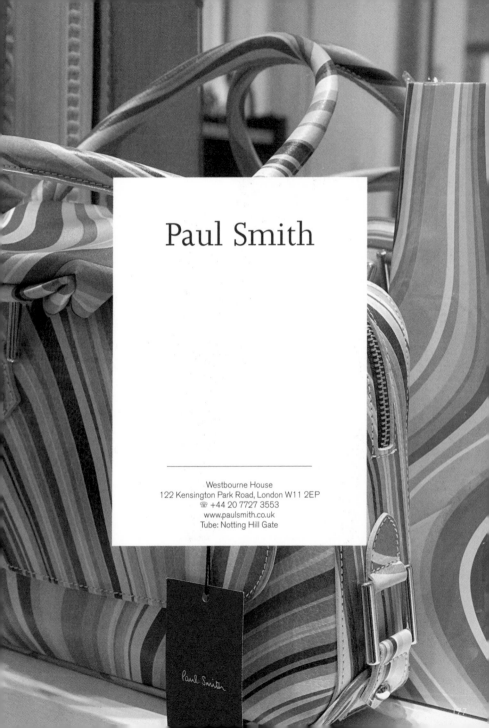

Paul Smith

Westbourne House
122 Kensington Park Road, London W11 2EP
☎ +44 20 7727 3553
www.paulsmith.co.uk
Tube: Notting Hill Gate

Melt

59 Ledbury Road, London W11 2AA
☎ +44 20 7727 5030
www.meltchocolates.com
Tube: Notting Hill Gate

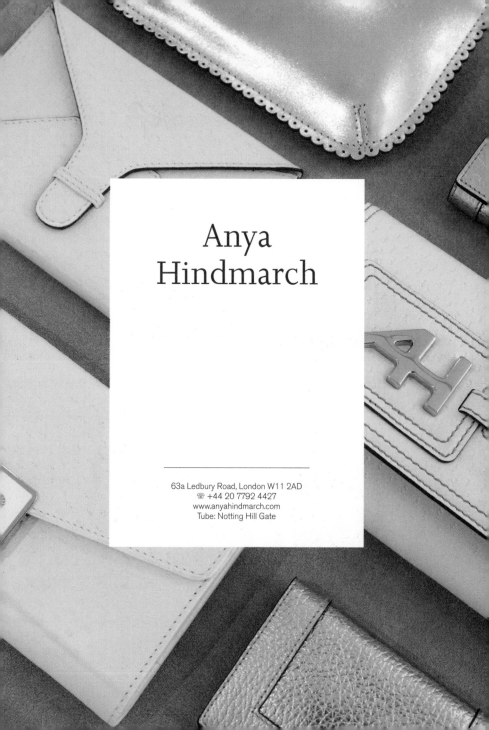

Anya
Hindmarch

63a Ledbury Road, London W11 2AD
☎ +44 20 7792 4427
www.anyahindmarch.com
Tube: Notting Hill Gate

Paul Smith

Westbourne House
122 Kensington Park Road
London W11 2EP
☎ +44 20 7727 3553
www.paulsmith.co.uk

pp. 176/177

Melt

59 Ledbury Road
London W11 2AA
☎ +44 20 7727 5030
www.meltchocolates.com

pp. 182/183

British Designer Fashion
Interior: Grand

Open: Mon–Fri 10am–6pm, Sat till 6.30pm | **X-Factor:** The accessories and the Home Collection.
Sir Paul Smith presents his fashion in a huge villa on three levels – an individual, very English mix.

Öffnungszeiten: Mo–Fr 10–18, Sa bis 18.30 Uhr |
X-Faktor: Die Accessoires und die Home Collection.
In einer riesigen Villa präsentiert Sir Paul Smith auf drei Etagen seine Mode – eigenwillig gemischt und sehr englisch.

Horaires d'ouverture : Lun–Ven 10h–18h, Sam jusqu'à 18h30 | **Le « petit plus » :** Les accessoires et la home collection.
Dans son immense villa Sir Paul Smith présente sur trois étages une mode éclectique et très british.

Heavenly Handmade Chocolate
Interior: Milk-white minimalist

Open: Mon–Sat 9am–6pm, Sun 11am–4pm | **X-Factor:** You can watch the chocolatiers at work.
Melt makes its clients do just that: these handmade sweets are a pure delight – especially the truffles with jasmine tea.

Öffnungszeiten: Mo–Sa 9–18, So 11–16 Uhr | **X-Faktor:** Man kann den Chocolatiers zuschauen.
Melt lässt seine Kunden dahinschmelzen: Die hausgemachten Süßigkeiten sind Genuss pur – vor allem die Trüffel mit Jasmintee.

Horaires d'ouverture : Lun–Sam 9h–18h, Dim 11h–16h | **Le « petit plus » :** On peut voir les chocolatiers à l'œuvre.
Melt fait fondre ses clients : les confiseries maison sont un pur délice, surtout les truffes au thé au jasmin.

Anya Hindmarch

63a Ledbury Road
London W11 2AD
☎ +44 20 7792 4427
www.anyahindmarch.com

pp. 186/187

Fashionable Bags
Interior: Luxurious

Open: Mon–Sat 10.30am–6pm, Tue till 7pm | **X-Factor:** The playful "Be a Bag" collection.
You simply cannot have enough handbags, as those London society girls who have fallen for Anya Hindmarch's models know only too well.

Öffnungszeiten: Mo–Sa 10.30–18, Di bis 19 Uhr |
X-Faktor: Die verspielte „Be a Bag"-Kollektion.
Handtaschen kann man nie genug haben! Das wissen auch die Londoner Society-Girls, die sich in Anya Hindmarchs Modelle verliebt haben.

Horaires d'ouverture : Lun–Sam 10h30–18h, Mar jusqu'à 19h | **Le « petit plus » :** La collection ludique « Be a Bag ».
On n'a jamais assez de sacs à main ! C'est ce que pensent aussi les society girls de Londres, qui sont toutes folles des modèles d'Anya Hindmarch.

Marble Arch

Oxford Street Bond Street

So Molton St
New
Bond Street

North Audley St
Davies
Brook

Park

Street

Grosvenor Street

SMYTHSON

Conduit St.

Upper Brook St

Grosvenor

STELLA
McCARTNEY
MATTHEW
WILLIAMSON

Carlos Pl

Square

Brutons Street

HOLLAND
& HOLLAND

Street

Mount

South Audley Street

JAMES PURDEY
& SONS

Berkeley Square

Farm Street

Hay's Mews

Berkeley Street

South St

Waverton St

Charles street

Deanery St

Lane

Curzon Street

Half Moon Street

HYDE
PARK

Hertford St

Old Park La

Piccadilly

Green
Park

GREEN
PARK

Hyde Park
Corner

Hyde Park Corner

Knightsbridge

Witton Pl

JIMMY
CHOO

Grosvenor Cres

Grosvenor Pl

Constitution Hill

BUCKINGHAM
PALACE

© MICHAEL A HILL

Mayfair